The Round Eye Dim Sum Cookbook

Mark Gargus

Illustrations by Mónica Montes

Copyright © 2012 Mark Gargus
All rights reserved.
ISBN-13 978-1480297609

Foreward

I have been fascinated with Asian culture and cuisine since I was a young child living in a rural area of the upper Midwest. After moving south to Birmingham, Alabama, I would visit friends in Atlanta, Georgia. When most people think of food and Atlanta, the upscale establishments in Midtown and Buckhead come to mind. Sadly overlooked by many, is the diverse cuisine found north of the city along Buford Highway – Latin, Chinese, Korean and more. This was where I was first introduced to Dim Sum – "Love at first bite".

Birmingham lacks such wonderful places to dine on such delicacies; but having a large Asian population, has many Asian markets. I thought to myself, "I am going to learn how to do this", while also believing that such a task was probably impossible for round eye to pull off.

Over the last eight years I have made Dim Sum at least once a month; sometimes two to three times a month. From serving just two, to a party of twenty with over twelve courses, I concluded "It can be done". It's not that hard, and with practice it's easy; and very impressive to family and friends. Enjoy.

Warmest Regards
Mark

Contents

Shao Mai	2
Chicken	2
Meat	3
Shrimp and Meat	3
Pearl Balls	4
Spinach with Ginger Dumplings	6
Rooster Dumplings	8
Scallops with Garlic and Black Beans	9
Barbecued Pork	10
Buns	12
Vegetable	13
Barbecued Pork – 1st Version	13
Barbecued Pork – 2nd Version	14
Red Bean Paste	14
Chicken	15
Clams in Black Bean Sauce	16
Vegetable with Oyster Sauce	16
Pork Swallows	18
Fried Money Bags	20
Shrimp Toast	22
Golden Shrimp Balls	24
Pot Stickers	26
1st Version	26
2nd Version	27
Oily Scallion Cakes	28
Spring Rolls	30

Stuffed Mushrooms with Oyster Sauce	32
Wontons	34
Dry Fried Beef	35
Stuffed Cucumbers	37
Spicy Cabbage	38
Egg Drop Soup	38
Wonton Soup	38
Fried Wonton Wrappers	39
Crunchy Soybeans in Spicy Sauce	39
Fried Rice	40
Homemade Wrappers	41
Wonton	41
Shao Mai	41
Spring Roll	42
Pot Sticker	43
Dipping Sauces	44
Sweet Thai Chili Sauce	44
Thai Hot Chili	44
Hoisin	44
Seasoned Soy	44
Soy Vinegar	44
Ginger Soy - 1st Version	44
Ginger Soy - 2nd Version	45
Oily Scallion Cake	45
Lime and Cilantro	45
Sweet and Sour	46
Hot Pepper Flakes in Oil	46

Introduction

Menu Planning
The heart of Dim Sum is variety. You should have different flavors and textures. For just a few people four dishes suffice. For example a vegetable dish, some fried rice, one steamed and one fried item – or two steamed and two fried items. For a large group, I plan on as almost many dishes as guests. Two to four pieces of each dish are a typical serving – as such, you may need to cut recipes in half. Dipping sauces (at the end of the book) are also essential. Most Dim Sum cookbooks recommend a particular sauce for each dish. I prefer to make no such recommendations, just have a variety available.

Ahead of Time
As seemingly daunting the menu planning may seem, most all of the fillings can be prepared in advance (hours to the night before), refrigerated and placed in the wrappers before cooking. The same applies to dipping sauces, though they should be brought to room temperature before serving. Dishes like barbecued pork and dry-fried beef can also be prepared in advance.
The fried items can also be frozen as follows. Arrange the uncooked wontons, shrimp toast, etc. on a non-stick baking sheet and place in freezer. When frozen, they can be put in a freezer bag and stored frozen for a month or so. When ready to cook, remove as many pieces as needed. If not defrosted, lower the recommended oil temperature by about 25°, and fry somewhat longer.

Assistance
Particularly with large parties, having an assistant who can hand ingredients to the chef and serve the guests can be very helpful

Serving

It is possible to have everything ready at once, but in a large Dim Sum restaurant, servers are passing by every few minutes with carts featuring 2-4 different dishes. To replicate the experience at home, it is best to present one or two dishes at a time, as they are ready. Note to the chef – reserve a few pieces of each dish for you to munch on while preparing subsequent items. As guests will devour everything presented, failure to observe this note will result in a hungry chef.

Steamed Dishes

You will need a steamer. Many Chinese cookbooks refer to bamboo steamers which look nice and do work, but most serious oriental cooks prefer the several layer stainless steel type. They hold more food, heat faster, are less likely to run dry, and are easier to clean. Mine are about 12" in diameter with 2 layers of racks.

Placement of food in the steamer is the next consideration. Some cooks use one plate, a large piece of parchment paper, or parchment cut into individual pieces for each item. The individual pieces are usually the best choice unless otherwise specified in the recipe. Wax paper can be used in lieu of parchment.

Fried Dishes

I use a wok along with an oil/candy thermometer, though a deep-fryer with temperature control would also work. Correct oil temperature, recommended in the recipes, is the key to a perfect dish. Oil not hot enough will result in a greasy, soggy product. Oil too hot will result in burnt wrappers or undercooked filling.

Time Saving Hint

Most dishes consist of ground meat(s), combined with finely chopped vegetables. If you have a meat grinder attachment for your heavy duty mixer or a food processor you can speed up the prep considerably. Just cut the meat and vegetables into small pieces along with any seasonings, mix well, and pulse in the food processor or run through the meat grinder. You can then ignore the ground meat and finely chopped instructions in the recipes.

· 1 ·

Shao Mai

There are countless variations of this dim sum staple. Following are several of my favorites. Feel free to experiment. Each makes approximately two dozen shao mai. Square wonton wrappers work fine, but in well stocked oriental grocery, you may find shao mai wrappers which look similar, but are thinner, giving the final product less of a "doughy" texture.

    24 wonton or shao mai wrappers

Prepare one more fillings.

Place a shy Tbsp of filling in the center of wrapper. Gather the edges the wrapper over the filling, leaving them open on top, sort of like a paper grocery bag. Then lightly tap bottom and place on parchment squares.

Steam over boiling water for 10-14 minutes.

Chicken

    1 lb chicken, ground or finely chopped
    4 fresh water chestnuts or jicama (about ¼ cup), finely chopped
    1 small carrot, finely chopped
    2 scallions, finely chopped
    1 tsp ginger, finely chopped
    1 tsp sesame oil
    1 tsp rice wine or dry sherry
    1 tsp soy sauce
    Pinch salt
    1 tsp sugar
    1 tsp cornstarch

Combine all ingredients and mix well

Meat

    1 lb pork or beef, ground or finely chopped
    1 Tbsp rice wine or dry sherry
    2 Tbsp light soy sauce
    1 scallion, finely chopped
    Pinch of salt
    4 fresh water chestnuts or equivalent jicama (about $\frac{1}{4}$ cup), finely chopped

Combine all ingredients and mix well.

Shrimp and Meat (Street Vendor Dumplings)

    6-8 dried Chinese black mushrooms, reconstituted in boiling water, squeezed of excess water, stems removed and finely chopped
    6 oz cleaned shrimp, ground or finely chopped
    12 oz pork, ground or finely chopped
    4 scallions, finely chopped
    Pinch salt
    $1\frac{1}{2}$ tsp sugar
    $1\frac{1}{2}$ Tbsp oyster sauce
    $1\frac{1}{2}$ Tbsp cornstarch

Combine all ingredients and mix well.

Pearl Balls

- 1 cup raw rice, preferably glutinous, but any short grain white rice will do
- 1 lb pork, ground or finely chopped
- 4 scallions, finely chopped
- 4 fresh water chestnuts or jicama (about ¼ cup), finely chopped
- Pinch salt
- 2 cloves garlic, finely chopped
- 2 tsp ginger, finely chopped
- 1 tsp sesame oil
- 2 tsp light soy sauce
- 2 tsp rice wine or dry sherry

Soak the rice for 30 minutes in cold water, drain well in a strainer and spread out on a plate to dry.

Combine other ingredients and mix well.

Divide mixture into 20 portions roll into little balls. Roll meatballs in rice until coated.

Place on parchment squares and steam for 30 minutes.

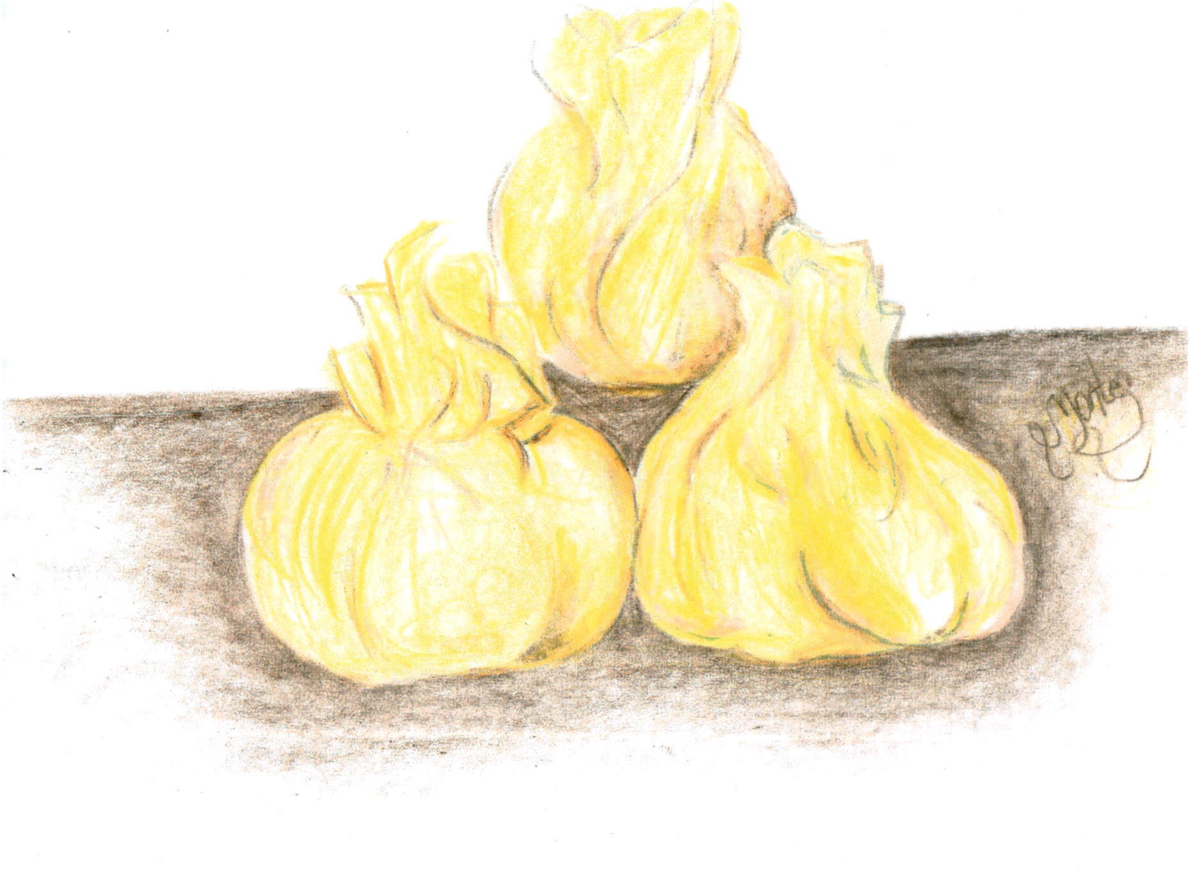

Spinach with Ginger Dumplings

    1 Tbsp ginger, finely chopped
    2 cloves garlic, finely chopped
    8-10 oz cleaned and chopped spinach
    15-20 wonton wrappers

Heat 1½ Tbsp of vegetable oil in your wok over medium heat. Add garlic and ginger and fry 1 minute.

Add the spinach stir-fry 2 minutes. You may wish to give it a pinch of salt just before ready to remove. Set aside and let it cool.

Place a shy Tbsp of spinach mixture in center of a wonton. Slightly dampen the edges with a little water. Carefully pull up edges and twist the top closed – should look kind of like a little mojo bag. Place on parchment squares and steam for 10 minutes.

·7·

Rooster Dumplings

- 8 oz chicken, ground or finely chopped
- 4 scallions, finely chopped
- 1 tsp ginger, finely chopped
- 4 fresh water chestnuts or jicama (about ¼ cup), finely chopped
- 2 Tbsp bamboo shoots, finely chopped
- 2 tsp rice wine or dry sherry
- 1 tsp salt
- 1 tsp sugar
- 1 tsp light soy sauce
- 1 tsp sesame oil
- 1 Tbsp oyster sauce
- 1 Tbsp cornstarch
- 16 round wonton wrappers (can be cut from square wonton or square egg roll wrappers)

Combine all ingredients except wrappers and mix well

Place 2 tsp of filling in the center of wrapper, fold in half. Then pinch edges together, using a little water on edges to help them seal well. The top should be crimped by pinching and look fan like.

They can be cooked in boiling water for 5-7 minutes, or placed on parchment and steamed for 8-10 minutes.

Scallops with Garlic and Black Beans

    1 lb scallops
    2 Tbsp vegetable oil
    3-5 cloves garlic
    1 Tbsp fermented black beans
    1½ tsp ginger
    1-1½ Tbsp oyster sauce
    2 tsp soy sauce
    1 Tbsp gin, rice wine or dry sherry
    1½ tsp rice wine vinegar
    1 tsp sugar
    Pinch of white or black pepper
    Pinch of salt

Thinly slice 2-3 cloves of the garlic and fry in the oil until lightly browned. Remove garlic and set aside. Pour 1 Tbsp of the garlic oil over the scallops.

Place the beans in a strainer and rinse well under running water – allow to drain. Failure to rinse thoroughly will result in an inedibly salty dish.

Mince the ginger and remaining garlic.

Combine the beans, ginger, garlic, oyster sauce, rice wine, vinegar, sugar, pepper and salt – mix well. Add scallops with their garlic oil and coat them well. Let sit for 15-20 minutes.

Place scallops on a heat proof plate or shallow bowl. Place plate in a steamer for 5-7 minutes covered. Carefully remove plate from steamer and put fried garlic flakes on top of scallops and serve.

Barbecued Pork

As well as delicious by itself, a portion can be used for making barbecued pork filling for buns.
- 1 lb ½" thick boneless pork chops or pork tenderloin cut to about the same size
- 2 Tbsp honey
- 3 Tbsp light soy sauce
- 1 tsp dark soy sauce
- 1 Tbsp rice wine or dry sherry
- 1 clove garlic, finely chopped

Combine all of the ingredients in a shallow dish. Let pork marinade 2 hours, turning and coating every 30 minutes or so.

Preheat oven to 425°

Use steel skewers through the pork chop size pieces and hang them over a roasting pan filled with about ½" water. Roast for 20 minutes, basting with drippings and leftover marinade every 5 minutes or so. Reduce to 325° and roast about 5 minutes more.

Slice diagonally against the grain into ¼" wide pieces.

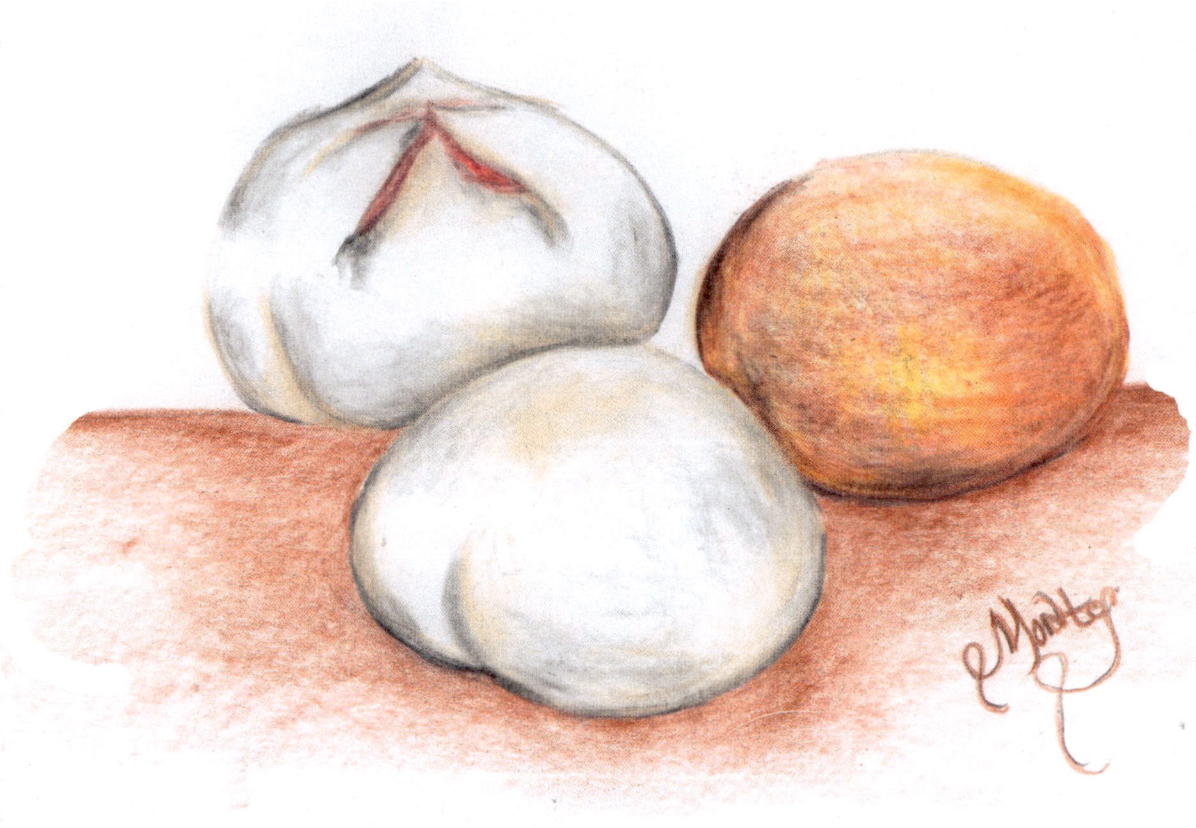

Buns

This recipe works well for steamed or baked buns. Steamed buns are more traditional, though since they do not brown, they look a little unusual to western eyes. You will be surprised at how delicious and different they are. Often I will make some steamed and others baked. Following the dough recipe are several filling suggestions. If you run out of filling mixture, some plain buns are nice, too.

- 1 packet (2¼ tsp) dried yeast
- 1 cup lukewarm water
- 4½ cups flour
- ¼ cup sugar
- 2 Tbsp Crisco or vegetable oil
- ½ cup boiling water

Dissolve yeast in lukewarm water. Add 1 cup flour, mix well and cover with damp cloth. Let rise until bubbles have formed, at least 30 minutes.

Dissolve sugar and vegetable oil in ½ cup boiling water. When cooled to lukewarm, pour into yeast mixture and work in 3½ cups flour.

Knead dough on lightly floured board until smooth. Put in large greased bowl in warm place to rise until about doubled in size, about an hour.

While the dough is rising, prepare one or more fillings.

Then divide dough in half. Take first portion and knead for 2 minutes. Roll into 12"x 2" cylinder. Cut cylinder into 12 pieces. Repeat with other half.

Roll dough pieces into 3"-4" circles. Add 1½-2 tsp of filling in center of dough gently pull up edges and pinch together. Place pinched side down on parchment squares or baking sheet. Sprinkle with white or black sesame seeds if desired. Let the finished buns rise 30 minutes or so, while you are working on other projects.

Steam over boiling water for 10-12 minutes or bake in 350° oven for 15-20 minutes until golden brown. For steamed buns, sometimes you may wish to cut a small "X" in the top with sharp scissors to expose some of the filling. If your first attempts aren't pretty don't freak out, they will be very tasty. With practice they'll be gorgeous.

Vegetable

- 1 tsp ginger, finely chopped
- 2 cloves garlic, finely chopped
- 1 cup coarsely chopped bok choy
- ⅓ cup bean sprouts or ¼ cup shredded bamboo shoots
- 1 small carrot, finely chopped
- 1 tsp sesame oil
- 2 Tbsp Thai sweet chili sauce

Heat 2 Tbsp oil in wok over medium heat. When hot, add ginger and garlic and stir-fry 30 seconds. Add vegetables stir-fry 2 minutes. Remove from heat. Stir in sesame oil and chili sauce. Let cool.

Barbecued Pork – 1st version

- 1 scallion, finely chopped
- 1 clove garlic, finely chopped
- 2 Tbsp light soy sauce
- 2 Tbsp oyster sauce
- 1 Tbsp sugar
- 1 Tbsp cornstarch
- 2 Tbsp of water
- ½ lb barbecued pork cut into small cubes

In a small bowl, mix soy, oyster sauce and sugar. In another bowl mix cornstarch and water.

Heat 2 Tbsp oil in wok, until nearly smoking. Add scallion and garlic and stir-fry for 20 seconds. Add pork and stir-fry for 30 seconds. Add sauce mixture stir 1 minute. Give the cornstarch mixture a stir, add, and stir a few seconds until it turns clear.

Remove from heat and let cool.

Barbecued Pork - 2nd version

  1 Tbsp oyster sauce
  1 tsp dark soy
  2 tsp ketchup
  2 tsp sugar
  Pinch of black or white pepper
  2 tsp cornstarch
  5 Tbsp chicken stock
  1/3 cup onion, finely chopped
  3/4 cup barbecued pork cut into small cubes
  1½ tsp rice wine, gin, or dry sherry
  ½ tsp sesame oil

In a small bowl, combine oyster sauce, soy, ketchup, sugar, pepper, stock and cornstarch.
Heat 1 Tbsp oil in wok until nearly smoking. Add onion, lower heat to medium stir-fry for 3 minutes. Add pork cubes stir-fry 1 minute. Add wine and mix well. Add sauce mixture stir until sauce thickens and has a nice brown color. Add sesame oil and mix.
Remove from heat and let cool.

Red Bean Paste

  1 can sweet red bean paste
Open can. Now how easy is that?

Chicken

    4 dried Chinese black mushrooms
    2 tsp ginger, finely chopped
    8 oz chicken, ground or finely chopped
    2 Tbsp bamboo shoots or jicama, finely chopped
    3 scallions, finely chopped
    1 Tbsp oyster sauce
    1 tsp soy sauce
    ½ tsp sesame oil
    1 Tbsp of cornstarch mixed with equal amount of water

Cover the mushrooms with boiling water for 20 minutes, drain, remove stems and chop into match head size pieces.

Heat about 1-1½ Tbsp of vegetable oil in your wok.

Add ginger and stir-fry for 30 seconds. Add chicken and stir-fry for about 2 minutes until the chicken changes color and stiffens some. Then add the remaining ingredients except cornstarch and water. Stir-fry 1-2 more minutes and add the cornstarch and water. When the sauce thickens, remove and let cool.

Clams in Black Bean Sauce

    1 lb fresh clams in shell, rinsed
    2 cloves garlic, finely chopped
    2 tsp ginger, finely chopped
    2 tsp fermented black beans
    2 Tbsp soy sauce
    ¼ cup water
    2 Tbsp oyster sauce

Place the beans in a strainer and rinse well under running water. Allow to drain and lightly mash. Failure to rinse thoroughly will result in an inedibly salty dish.

In a small sauce pan heat 2 tsp of oil. Add garlic and ginger cook about 30 seconds or so. Add the black beans, soy sauce, water and oyster sauce. After 30 seconds or so, turn off heat. Steam clams for about 4 minutes. Throw away any that didn't open. Open clams and reheat sauce. Pour sauce over clams and serve

Vegetable with Oyster Sauce

Traditionally made with a bunch of blanched garlic chives, the sauce works well with many vegetables – snow peas, broccoli, asparagus and more.

    12oz vegetable of your choice
    2 Tbsp oyster sauce
    3 Tbsp chicken stock
    2 tsp soy sauce
    1 tsp sesame oil
    1 tsp of cornstarch mixed with 1 Tbsp of stock or water.

Boil or steam vegetable of your choice until al dente.
Bring remaining ingredients to a boil. When bubbling and thick, pour over vegetable and serve.

·17·

Pork Swallows

    8 oz pork, ground or finely chopped
    4 oz cleaned shrimp, ground or finely chopped
    1 Tbsp ginger, finely chopped
    4 scallions, finely chopped
    2 tsp rice wine or dry sherry
    Pinch salt
    1 tsp sesame oil
    2 tsp cornstarch
    20 square wonton wrappers

Combine all ingredients (except the wonton wrappers) in a bowl and mix well.
Place 2 tsp of filling in the center of a wonton wrapper. Slightly dampen the edges with a little water. Take two points diagonal from each other and pinch. Then repeat with the other two. They will meet in the center leaving four edges. The edges will be sloping down from the center. Pinch the edges until completely sealed. Repeat with remaining wontons and filling.
Heat a wok with oil deep enough for deep frying, to 350°.
Working in small batches carefully place dumpling pointy side down in the oil. They will flip around don't worry about it. Fry until golden brown about 1-2 minutes. Use slotted spoon to remove. Drain on paper towels.
Place in warm (200°-220°) oven, if needed.

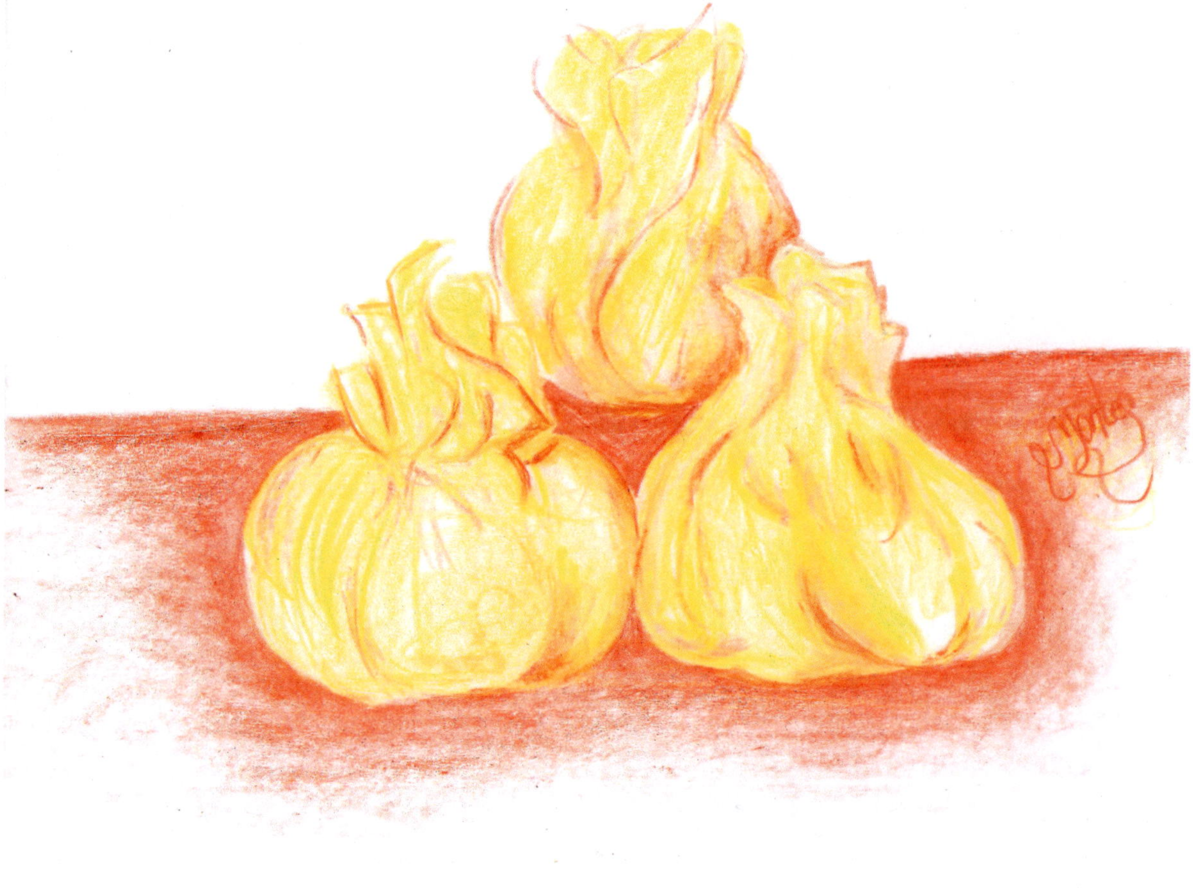

Fried Money Bags

- 1 small bunch bok choy
- 8 oz chicken, ground or finely chopped
- 1 tsp sesame oil
- 3 scallions, finely chopped
- 1 tsp ginger, finely chopped
- 1 clove garlic, finely chopped
- 1 tsp rice wine or dry sherry
- 2 tsp oyster sauce
- 1 tsp light soy sauce
- 2 tsp cornstarch
- 20 wonton wrappers

Separate the bok choy leaves, parboil for one minute. Coarsely chop the bok choy combine with remaining ingredients (except the wontons).

Place 2 tsp of filling in the center of a wonton. Slightly dampen the edges with a little water. Carefully pull up edges and twist the top closed – should look kind of like a little mojo bag. Heat wok with enough oil for deep frying to 350°-375°. Working with a few at a time, deep fry money bags 1-2 minutes until golden brown. Use slotted spoon to remove. Drain on paper towels.

Place in warm (200°-220°) oven, if needed.

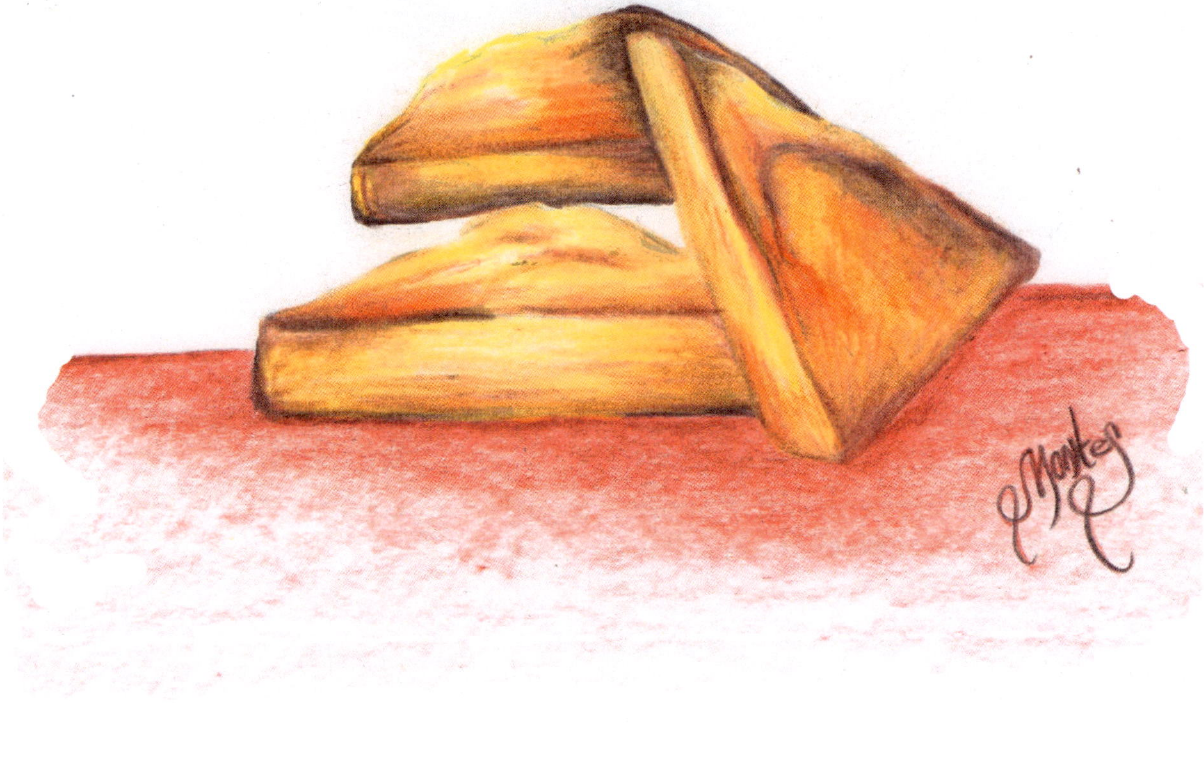

Shrimp Toast

9-16 (depending on size) slices of thin dense white bread (slightly dried-out works best)
1 lb cleaned shrimp, ground or finely chopped
4 fresh water chestnuts or equivalent jicama (about ¼ cup), finely chopped
½ medium onion, finely chopped
1 scallion, finely chopped
½ tsp salt
1 tsp rice wine or dry sherry
1 Tbsp cornstarch
1 egg slightly beaten
¼ tsp pepper

Trim crust off bread. Cut large slices of bread into four triangles – smaller slices cut in half diagonally. Take 4 pieces of the bread, dip in water and squeeze out liquid. Tear into little pieces. In a bowl, combine moist bread pieces and remaining ingredients – mix well.

Take a triangle of dried bread, place a spoon of shrimp mixture and spread out but leaving slightly mounded – about ¼" thick in the center. Repeat with remainder.

Heat your wok with enough oil for deep-frying to 370°

When hot, place toast in oil, in batches, shrimp side down. When the bread starts browning, flip over and fry about 30 seconds to 1 minute more. Then when golden brown, use slotted spoon to remove. Drain on paper towels.

Place in warm (200°-220°) oven, if needed.

· 23 ·

Golden Shrimp Balls

Though different in appearance, the flavor and texture is very similar to Shrimp Toast.

    10 slices of thinly sliced white bread
    1 lb cleaned shrimp, ground or finely chopped
    6 fresh water chestnuts or equivalent jicama (about ⅓ cup), finely chopped
    2 strips bacon, finely chopped
    1 tsp sugar
    Pinch salt
    2 tsp cornstarch

Remove crusts and cut bread into tiny cubes. Put on a tray to dry out – a warm oven will expedite this.

In a bowl mix remaining ingredients and put in refrigerator to chill 10-15 minutes.

Roll a Tbsp of meat mixture into a ball. Roll meatball through bread cubes until coated. Place on tray and continue with the rest - or get someone else to do it!

Fill wok with enough oil for deep frying and heat to 375°. Working in batches fry shrimp balls 1-2 minutes until deep golden brown. Use slotted spoon to remove. Drain on paper towels. Place in warm (200°-220°) oven, if needed.

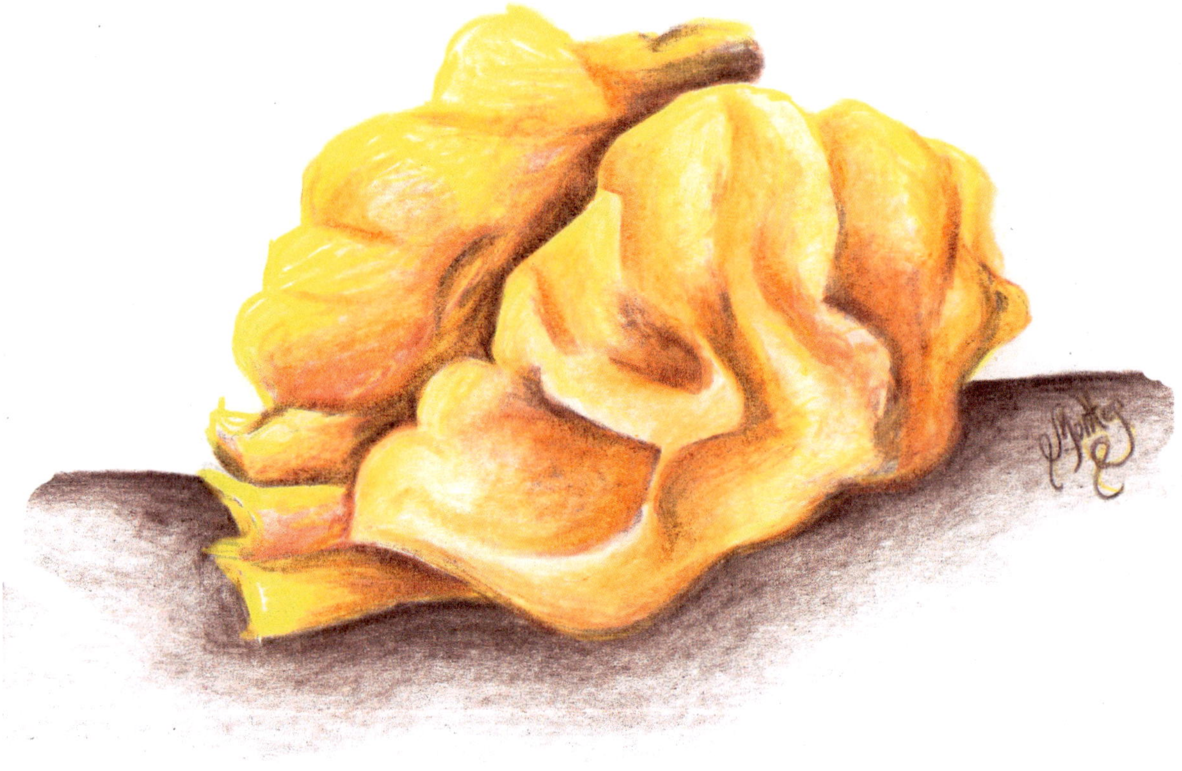

Pot Stickers

    24 pot sticker wrappers (3"-4" round wrappers)

Prepare one of the pot sticker fillings.

Place about 1 Tbsp of filling in center of wrapper. Slightly dampen the edges with a little water. Then pinch edges together, using a little water on edges to help them seal well. The top should be crimped by pinching and look fan like. Tap bottom to flatten.

A large skillet with lid is needed. A non-stick skillet is highly preferable to avoid the pot stickers really sticking.

Heat 1 Tbsp oil in skillet. Add the number of pot stickers you can cook at one time, without crowding or touching. Fry them about 3 minutes until the bottoms begin to brown. Have lid on hand to cover and protect yourself – it's going to act up a little. Add ½ cup water and cover. Reduce heat to low for 6 minutes. Carefully remove lid raise heat to high cook until water is gone and bottoms are brown and crispy looking.

Use spatula to remove to serving plate.

Place in warm (200°-220°) oven, if needed.

1st Version

    1 lb pork or beef, ground or finely chopped
    1 scallion, finely chopped
    1 tsp ginger, finely chopped
    4 oz cleaned shrimp, ground or finely chopped
    1 Tbsp oil
    ¼ tsp salt
    2 Tbsp soy sauce
    1 Tbsp rice wine or dry sherry
    Pinch of sugar
    ¼ cup chicken stock

Combine the ingredients in a bowl.

2nd Version

- 8oz shredded napa cabbage or bok choy
- 8 oz pork, ground or finely chopped
- 2 Tbsp ginger, finely chopped
- 1 scallion, finely chopped
- 2 tsp soy sauce
- 2 tsp rice wine or dry sherry
- ½ tsp sugar
- 1 Tbsp sesame oil
- 24 pot sticker wrappers (3"-4" round wrappers)

Lightly salt cabbage and set aside 10-15 minutes to wilt. Rinse well and squeeze out all excess liquid.

Combine the bok choy or napa cabbage and remaining ingredients in a bowl.

Oily Scallion Cakes

    3 cups all purpose flour
    1 cup water
    15 scallions, finely chopped
    1 tsp salt
    2 Tbsp vegetable shortening or lard
    Sesame oil
    Dipping sauce – see recipe in sauces

Mix in a bowl until a stiff dough forms the set aside for 30 minutes.

Lightly coat flat surface and rolling pin with sesame oil - use additional sesame oil should things begin to stick. Knead the dough and separate into two balls. Roll one dough ball into an 8" x 10" rectangle. Sprinkle about ½ tsp salt on the rectangle and press into the dough with fingers. Spread about 1 Tbsp lard or shortening over the surface of the dough. Sprinkle half the scallions on top the rectangle. Roll the dough up like a jellyroll, pinching the ends. Divide the roll into 3 sections and pinch the ends of each section so that the scallions don't fall out. Follow this same procedure for the other balls of the dough. Everything can be completed to this point, up to several hours in advance.

Place ⅛" of vegetable oil in a flat skillet and heat until almost smoking.

Place one of the scallion cake balls on the oiled flat surface, pinched ends on top and bottom and smash it into a pancake, 5"-6" in diameter. Peel from the surface and place in the hot oil in the skillet. Let each cake fry for about 3 minutes on each side, then remove and blot with paper towel. Cut into wedges and serve immediately as they come out of the pan, with dipping sauce on the side.

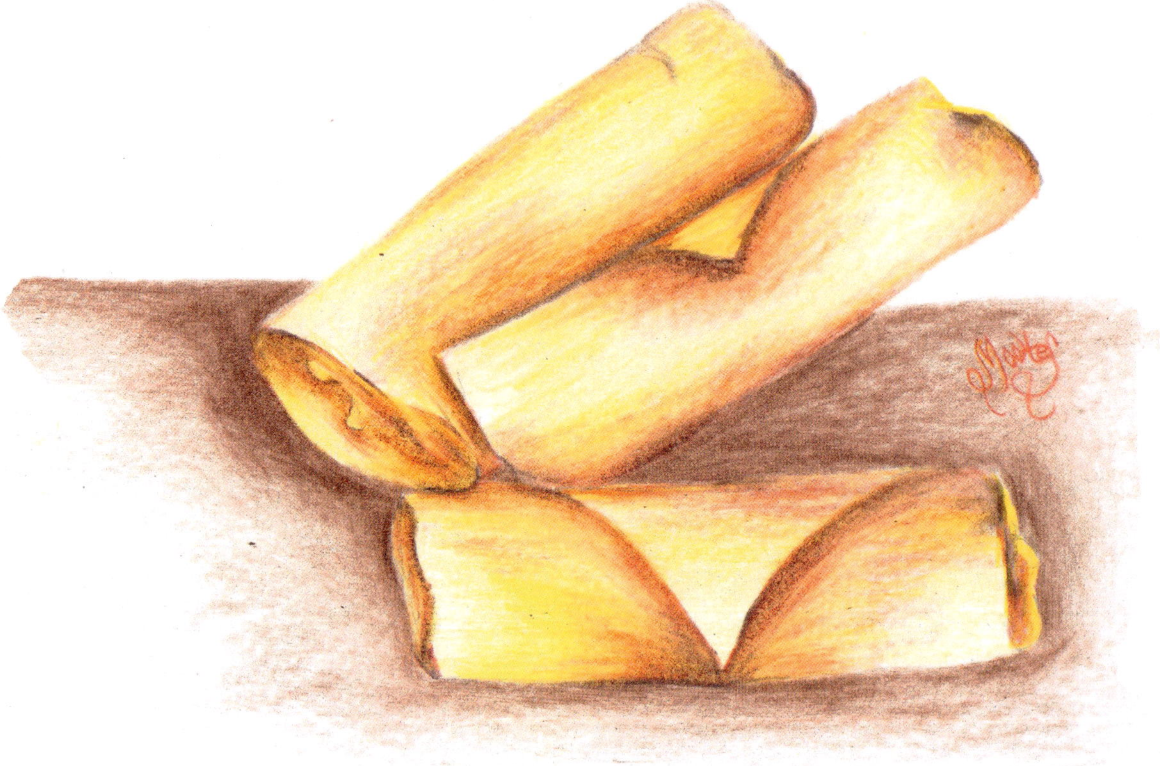

Spring Rolls

- 2 oz pork, ground or finely chopped
- 2 oz cleaned shrimp, ground or finely chopped
- 2 tsp soy sauce
- 2 tsp rice wine or dry sherry
- 1 tsp sesame oil
- ½ tsp sugar
- 1 cup bean sprouts
- 1 cup shredded napa cabbage or bok choy
- ¼ cup bamboo shoots, finely chopped
- ¼ cup mushrooms of your liking, finely chopped
- 3 scallions, roughly chopped
- 1 clove garlic, finely chopped
- 1 tsp cornstarch mixed with 1 Tbsp water
- 8 6" spring roll (egg roll) wrappers

Mix together the soy, rice wine, sesame oil and sugar. Pour half of it over the pork, the other half over the shrimp.

Combine the vegetables and garlic in another bowl.

Heat wok, add 2 Tbsp of oil. When hot add pork stir-fry 1 minute. Add shrimp and stir-fry 1 minute more. Remove to a clean bowl and wipe out wok.

Heat wok add 2 more Tbsp of oil. When hot add the veggies. Stir-fry 2 minutes then return meat and shrimp to wok. When everything is well mixed, add cornstarch and water mixture and stir-fry for 30 seconds.

Let everything cool. Pour off excess liquid, if any.

Spring Rolls (cont'd)

Place a spring roll wrapper on your working surface oriented in a diamond shape. Put an eighth of filling on wrapper about half way between the bottom tip and the middle. Spread filling evenly across the wrapper. Pull up bottom point to the center of the wrapper and roll it a little. Slightly dampen the exposed edges with a little water. Then fold over the outside edges and roll the rest of the way up. Do not roll or pack filling too tightly as it will not cook evenly.

Heat wok with a sufficient amount of oil for deep frying to 375°. Carefully place 2-3 spring rolls in oil at a time. Fry, turning occasionally, for 3-5 minutes until an even golden brown. Use slotted spoon to remove. Drain on paper towels.

Place in warm (200°-220°) oven, if needed.

Stuffed Mushrooms with Oyster Sauce

    15-20 dried Chinese black mushrooms
    ½ lb pork, beef, or cleaned shrimp (I prefer shrimp), ground or finely chopped
    Pinch of salt
    1 tsp oil
    ½ tsp sugar
    1 Tbsp rice wine or dry sherry
    1 Tbsp soy sauce
    1 tsp cornstarch plus some extra
    2 Tbsp oyster sauce

Pour 1½ cups of boiling water over the mushrooms. After 30 minutes or so, remove mushrooms saving 1 cup of the water. Remove the stems.
Mix the shrimp or meat with the salt, oil, sugar, rice wine, soy and tsp of cornstarch. Sprinkle a little cornstarch inside the mushrooms. Place about a Tbsp of meat mixture inside. Heat a skillet with 2 Tbsp of vegetable oil, when hot fry mushrooms filling side down until light brown. Gently turn mushrooms over. Add mushroom stock and cook about 10 more minutes. Add the oyster sauce. In about one minute, when the sauce thickens, it's done.

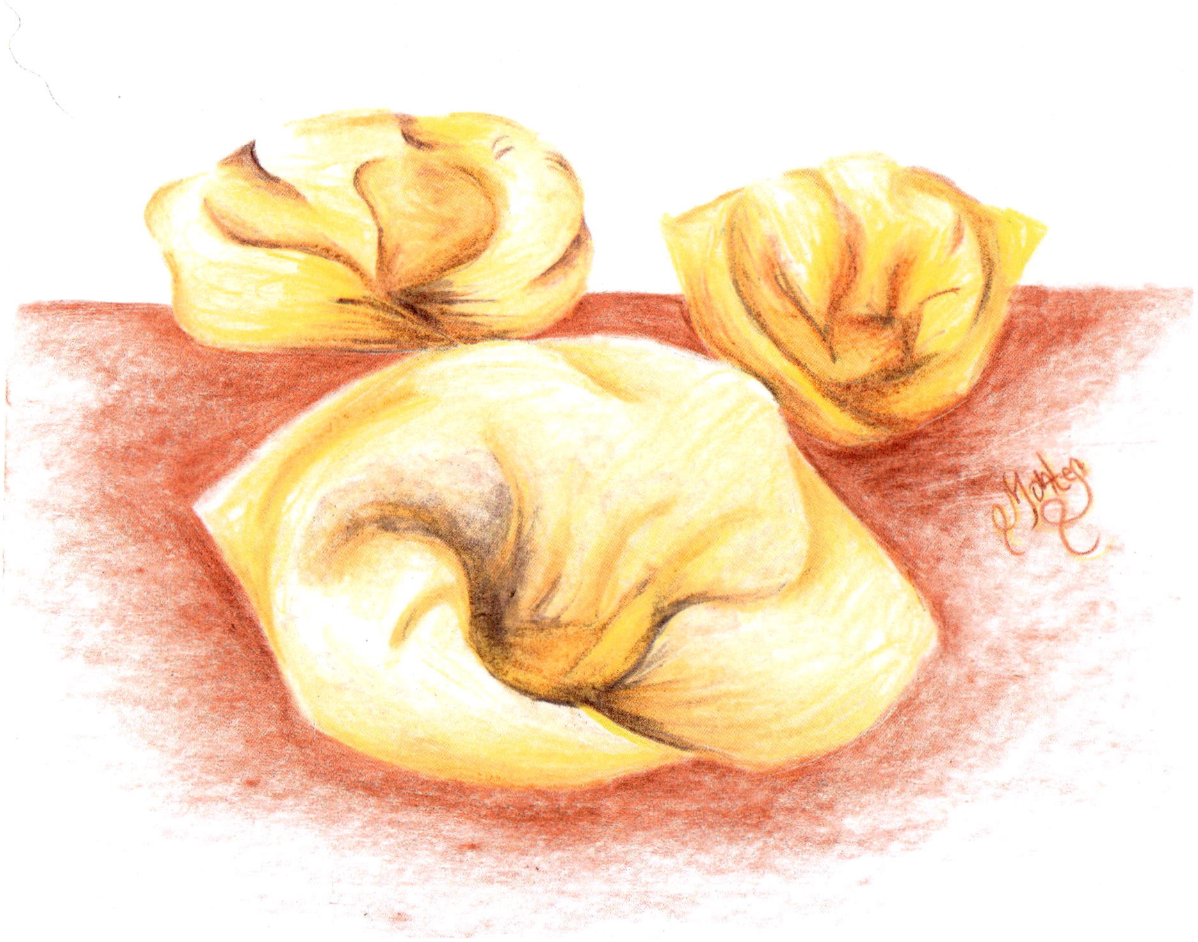

Wontons

These may be fried, boiled or steamed.

> ½ pound meat (pork, chicken, beef or cleaned shrimp), ground or finely chopped
> ¼ tsp salt
> 1 Tbsp soy sauce
> 1 Tbsp rice wine or dry sherry
> 4 fresh water chestnuts or equivalent jicama (about ¼ cup), finely chopped
> 1 scallion, finely chopped
> 1 egg beaten
> A couple of bok choy leaves, finely chopped
> 30 wonton wrappers

Combine the ingredients (except the wontons) in a bowl.

Place 1 tsp of filling in the center of wrapper. Slightly dampen the edges with a little water. Fold in half away from you, pinch closed, then fold the dough part in half again toward you. Pull outside edges together like a horseshoe shape and pinch edges together.

To fry, fill wok with enough oil for deep frying and heat to 375°. Working in batches fry wontons about 2 minutes. Use slotted spoon to remove. Drain on paper towels.

Place in warm (200°-220°) oven, if needed. Leftovers can be refried the next day.

To boil, bring a large pot of water (3-4 qt) to boil and add up to 15 wontons. Leaving heat on high, boil until they float on surface. Remove to strainer, rinse with cold water, drain and set aside. They can then be added to Egg Drop Soup (see recipe) and you have Wonton Soup.

They can also be placed on parchment and steamed for 10-15 minutes.

Dry-Fried Beef

    1 lb lean tough beef – top or bottom round
    2 scallions
    ½ Tbsp ginger, sliced into ⅛" shreds
    ½ tsp sugar
    3 Tbsp soy sauce
    1 Tbsp rice wine or dry sherry
    1½ tsp sesame oil
    1 tsp ground Szechwan peppercorns
    3 carrots
    4 stalks celery
    1½ tsp salt
    10 dried red chilies

Slice the beef into very thin slivers about 3" long and ¼" wide. Bruise one of the scallions with the side of a knife and cut into 1" lengths. Combine the beef, scallion, ginger, sugar, soy, rice wine, Szechwan peppercorns and ½ tsp of the sesame oil.

Cut the other scallion into very fine slivers about 2" long and set aside.

Peel and slice the carrots into shreds about the same size as the meat. Sprinkle with 1 tsp of the salt and set aside. After 15 minutes, pour off the brine and blot the carrots.

Slice the celery into shreds about the same size as the meat. Sprinkle with ½ tsp of the salt and set aside. After 5 minutes, pour off the brine and blot the celery.

Slice the chilies lengthwise into 2 or 3 strips.

Add 3 Tbsp oil to hot wok. Once oil is ready add the carrots by stir-frying over medium flame for about a minute. Then add the celery and stir-fry an additional 6 minutes or so. Remove carrots and celery and set aside. Wipe out wok.

Dry-Fried Beef (cont'd)

Remove the scallions from the beef marinade. Add 3 Tbsp oil to wok. When hot, add the red chilies. Immediately add the beef to the wok by stir-frying at high heat until all the liquid has evaporated – usually 10-15 minutes of cooking time. Lower the heat to about medium and stir-fry about another minute. Then add carrots and celery and stir-fry about another minute or so. Reduce the heat until it is barely flickering (assuming you use a gas range). Add the scallion slivers and cook over extremely low heat for about one hour. Occasionally flip the ingredients over during this time. This should result in a very dry mixture. Just prior to serving turn up the heat and add 1 tsp sesame oil. This can be prepared in advance and reheated at serving time.

Stuffed Cucumbers

One of my all time favorites. Easy to make, tasty and makes a great presentation.

    2-4 cucumbers
    1 tsp ginger, finely chopped
    3 scallions, finely chopped
    ½ lb pork, ground or finely chopped
    1 Tbsp soy sauce
    ½ tsp sesame oil
    ¼ tsp roasted ground Szechwan peppercorns
    1 egg
    1 Tbsp cornstarch
    ¼ tsp sesame oil

Peel, cut cucumbers in half crosswise and scoop out seeds with a spoon. Mix together the other ingredients, except for the last ¼ tsp of sesame oil. Stuff the cucumbers with meat mixture. Place on a plate. Steam for 20 minutes. Remove stuffed cucumbers to another plate. Make a sauce by combining the remaining ¼ tsp of sesame oil to the liquid on the steam plate. Cut cucumbers in ¼"-½" inch medallions and pour the sauce over top. Can be reheated over steam for a couple of minutes before serving.

Spicy Cabbage

    1 head medium cabbage or bok choy
    1 Tbsp of cornstarch
    ¾ cup water
    1 Tbsp of hot pepper paste

Combine the cornstarch and ¼ cup of water.
Remove the tough outer leaves from the cabbage, wash and cut into roughly 1" squares.
Heat 3 Tbsp of vegetable oil in your wok. When hot, add the pepper paste and stir. Add the chopped cabbage and stir-fry gently for 5 minutes. Add the remaining ½ cup of water and a bit of salt. Cover the wok with lid and reduce flame to medium let cabbage boil about 12 minutes. Remix the cornstarch and water add to the cabbage and stir for 15-20 seconds. When thickened it's ready to serve.

Egg Drop Soup

    4 eggs
    ½ cup scallions, thinly sliced
    1 qt chicken stock

Beat the eggs well, as when making an omelet.
Bring the stock to a boil and salt to taste.
Slowly drizzle the beaten eggs into the stock while stirring with a fork. Add the scallions. You may want to have some fried wontons as a garnish.

Wonton Soup

Follow the egg drop soup as above, adding some boiled wontons (see recipe). The fried wontons are unnecessary.

Fried Wonton Wrappers

A bowl of fried wontons are great as an appetizer or for munching between dishes as well as a nice garnish to egg drop soup.

 1 dozen or more wonton wrappers

Slice wrappers into ¼" strips and separate. Deep-fry just until starting to turn color. Remove and drain.

Crunchy Soybeans in Spicy Sauce

Though not a Dim Sum item per se, they are often served in Chinese drinking establishments. They are great appetizers or to nibble on between dishes.

 3 cloves garlic, smashed but left whole
 1 tsp ginger, coarsely chopped
 2 scallions, coarsely chopped
 1 tsp sugar
 ¼ tsp salt
 ½ sesame oil
 1½ tsp rice vinegar
 2 Tbsp soy sauce
 1 tsp hot pepper flakes in oil
 ⅓ cup water
 ¾ cup dry raw soybeans

Combine all the ingredients except the soybeans.
Rinse the soybeans well and drain.
Heat a dry wok over medium heat and add the soybeans. Toss them around occasionally until slightly brown – they will still be crunchy but less hard. Immediately dump them into the sauce ingredients and stir. Allow to sit for at least 30 minutes before serving. They will keep for several days.

Fried Rice

Not traditionally Dim Sum, but can be used to stretch the menu.

- 1½ cups rice
- 3 cups water
- 5 scallions, sliced into ⅛" pieces crosswise
- 3 eggs

Prepare the rice as usual. As this is typically done with "stale" rice, it's best to do this in advance – when the rice is done, spread onto a large pan or platter to dry for a few hours. Beat the eggs in a small bowl.

Pour 5 Tbsp peanut oil into hot wok. When the oil is ready, pour in the eggs, cook for 30 seconds flip as for an omelet then remove and set aside. Add the rice to the pan and stir-fry until every bit has been exposed to the oil. Return the eggs to the wok. Add the scallions and ½ tsp salt. Stir-fry for about 6 minutes until the rice is beginning to crisp.

Homemade Wrappers

A good Asian market will have all of the needed wrappers. If not, or if you like to do everything yourself, following are recipes. Though having been done by hand for millennia, an Italian pasta roller (whether standalone or a KitchenAid attachment) results in a better product, with much less effort. My machine has settings from 1 (thick) to 8 (very thin). Before stacking your finished wrappers, dust them with cornstarch (not flour) first, or they will stick to one another for sure.

Wonton

- ¾ cup flour
- ⅓ cup water
- Cornstarch

In a medium bowl mix the flour and water. When it comes together put on a floured work area and knead until smooth – about 3 minutes. Roll into a ball, lightly dust with flour and place back in the bowl and cover with a lightly damped towel. Let rest for about 15 minutes.

By hand

Roll in to a 12" log then cut in half to make two 6" cylinders. Roll each cylinder out to 12"x12".

Pasta roller

Separate the dough into manageable pieces – if you have a pasta machine, you'll know what I mean. Run through the pasta machine, number by number, up to 7.

Cut to desired shape and size. For round wrappers, using a glass or can is sometimes helpful. Keep finished and extra dough covered to prevent drying out.

Shao Mai

Same as basic wonton, but roll thinner or for machine, up to number 8.

Spring Roll

    1½ cups all purpose flour
    ½ tsp salt
    1 egg
    Enough water added to the egg to make ½ cup liquid

Mix together the dry ingredients.

Lightly beat the egg and water until well combined.

Add liquid ingredients to the dry and mix until they come together. You may need to add a bit of water from time to time as the dough is coming together. On a floured work surface knead until smooth about 3 minutes. .Roll into a ball, lightly dust with flour and place back in the bowl and cover with a lightly damped towel. Let rest for about 15 minutes.

By hand

    Roll into a 12" log then cut in half to make two 6" cylinders. Roll each cylinder out to 12". Cut each cylinder into eight pieces. Roll it out with a rolling pin large enough to make 6"x6" square wrappers.

Pasta roller

    Separate the dough into manageable pieces – if you have a pasta machine, you'll know what I mean. Run through the pasta machine, number by number, up to 7.

Cut off sides to make even looking wrappers. Keep finished and extra dough covered to keep from drying out.

Pot Sticker

Similar to wonton wrappers, though a bit thicker.

    2 cups flour
    $\frac{2}{3}$ cup lukewarm water

Mix the flour and water in a bowl with a fork or chopstick. On a floured work surface knead until smooth about 3 minutes. Cover with a damp cloth set aside 10 minutes. Roll into a thin log and cut into 24 pieces.

By hand
    Roll into 3"-4" circles

Pasta roller
    Roll into balls. Run through, trying to preserve circular shape, number by number, up to 5.

Dipping Sauces

No matter how excellent your steamed or fried dishes may be, they will be incomplete without dipping sauces. Variety is essential.

Sweet Thai Chili

Use out of the bottle. Try to avoid brands with added MSG.

Thai Hot Chili

Use out of the bottle. Try to avoid brands with added MSG.

Hoisin

Dilute with water, 2 parts hoisin to 1 part water.

Seasoned Soy

One, or at most two, of the following should suffice. Other options include adding 1 clove minced garlic and or ¼ tsp sesame to any of the recipes.

Soy Vinegar

¼ cup soy sauce
2 Tbsp rice wine or red vinegar
2 tsp sugar
1 scallion (green part only), finely chopped

Ginger Soy - 1st Version

1 Tbsp ginger, finely chopped
½ cup soy sauce
2 Tbsp Thai sweet chili sauce

Ginger Soy – 2nd Ver

    2 tsp ginger, finely chopped
    ½ cup soy sauce
    ½ scallion, finely chopped

Oily Scallion Cake

    ¼ cup soy sauce
    1 tsp sesame oil
    2 tsp rice vinegar
    ½ tsp ginger, finely chopped
    1 scallion, finely chopped

Lime and Cilantro

    2 Tbsp fish sauce
    2 Tbsp wine vinegar
    2 Tbsp lime juice
    ½ tsp sugar
    2 Tbsp cilantro, finely chopped

Sweet and Sour

If there is a commercial brand you like – fine. I find this more interesting.

    ¼ cup catsup
    ¼ cup sugar
    1 cup water
    ¼ cup rice wine vinegar
    2 Tbsp cornstarch dissolved in 2 Tbsp water
    1 Tbsp green pepper, finely chopped
    2 Tbsp canned pineapple chunks

Bring the catsup, sugar, water and vinegar to a boil. Reduce heat, add the cornstarch mixture simmer until thickened. Add the green pepper and pineapple chunks. Mix well.

Hot Pepper Flakes in Oil

Used as an ingredient and a condiment in many Chinese recipes. Keeps refrigerated for months.

    ¼ cup oil
    ¼ cup dried red pepper flakes, the ones used on pizza
    ½ tsp salt

Heat the oil in small saucepan until barely smoking. Remove from heat for 5 seconds and add pepper flakes. When the foaming subsides, add the salt.

Important note - hold your breath and step back after adding pepper flakes.

If you breathe the vapor as it foams you will not like the result. I know this from personal experience.

Made in the USA
Columbia, SC
17 July 2023